Cut & Fold
PAPER SPACESHIPS
That Fly

Michael Grater

Dover Publications, Inc.
New York

INSTRUCTIONS

These paper spaceships are easy to make and they really do fly. The only tools you will need are

scissors
transparent tape
cardboard
paper clips
ruler or other straightedge

Begin by cutting out one of the spaceships, following the heavy black outline as carefully as you can.

Next, protect your work table by covering it with a piece of cardboard. Lay the cutout on the cardboard and score along the fold lines (single or double dashed lines). Single dashed lines tell you to fold *back*, so that the lines remain visible to you. Double dashed lines tell you to fold *forward*, so that the lines get hidden in the fold. (See Figure A.)

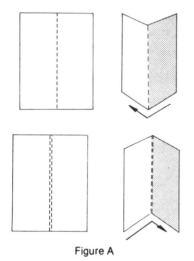

Figure A

Score single lines by laying a ruler next to them and drawing a scissors point along the whole length; apply some pressure, but not so much as to cut through the paper. Score double dashed lines *halfway* between the two.

After you've scored all the fold lines, fold them in sequence, following the order of the circled numbers. As you do this, refer to the explanatory diagrams that show you step-by-step how each spaceship is made, including when and how the tail plane is raised above the fuselage in some models. (See Figure B.) Note that to achieve the proper symmetry, the same folds are made on both wings. It is essential that all folds be made crisply and exactly where indicated.

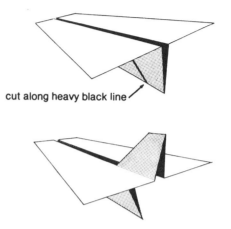

cut along heavy black line

Figure B

Before flying the spaceship, give the nose a little extra weight by adding a paper clip. You may also want to secure folds with little pieces of transparent tape. (See Figure C.)

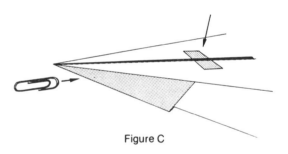

Figure C

Test fly the spaceship, increasing or decreasing the angle where the wings meet the fuselage until you find the dihedral that works best. If the spaceship corkscrews or spins when launched, the configuration of the wings is irregular because some of the folds have not been done precisely right. Correct this by unfolding and refolding more carefully.

EXPLANATORY DIAGRAMS FOLLOW PLATES

WARNING

Like any action toy, the models you will make from this book must be used carefully. Always make sure that you have a clear air space in front of you before flying, and *never* aim at a person or animal!

Copyright © 1980 by Michael Grater.
All rights reserved under Pan American and International Copyright Conventions.

Cut & Fold Paper Spaceships That Fly is a new work, first published by Dover Publications, Inc., in 1980.

International Standard Book Number: 0-486-23978-0
Library of Congress Catalog Card Number: 80-67099

Published in Canada by General Publishing Company, Ltd., 30 Lesmill Road, Don Mills, Toronto, Ontario.
Published in the United Kingdom by Constable and Company, Ltd.

Manufactured in the United States of America
Dover Publications, Inc.
31 East 2nd Street
Mineola, N.Y. 11501

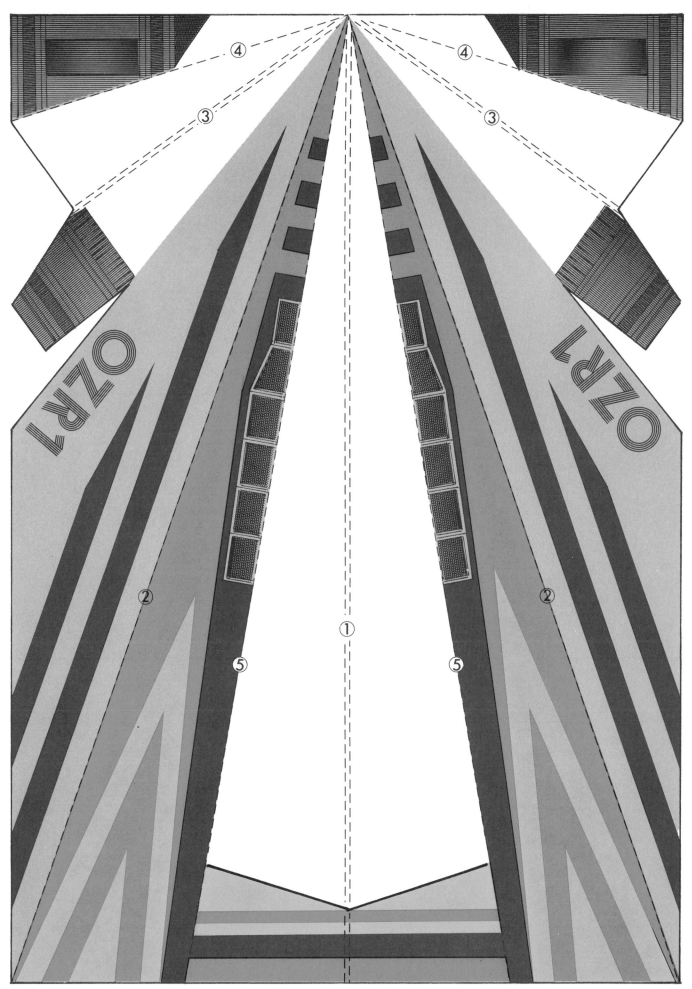

1. ORBITAL ZOOM RIDER

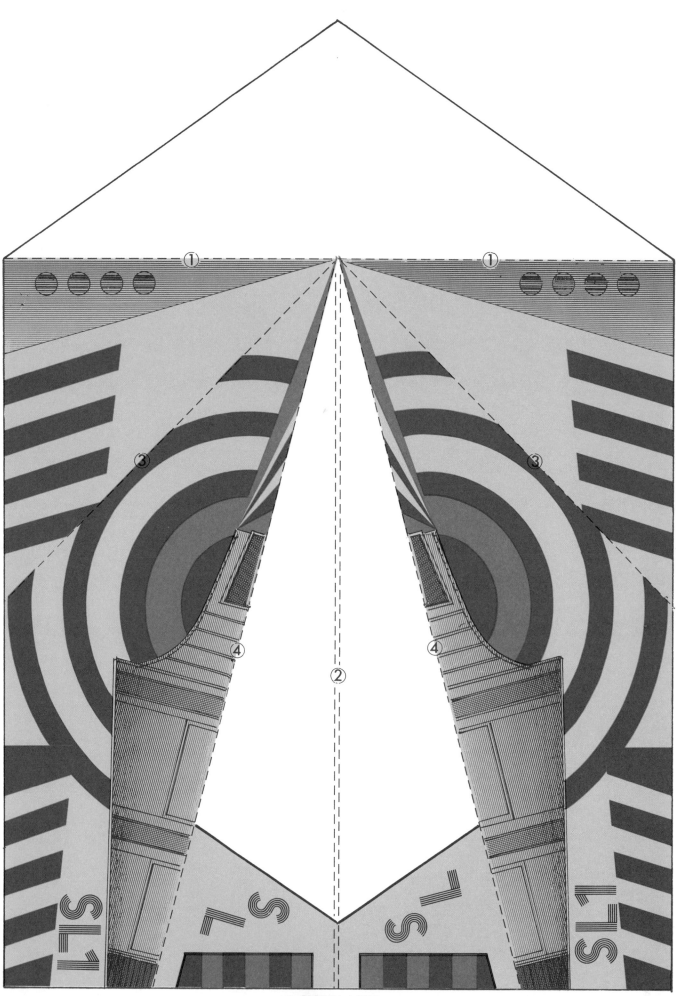

2. SIGNAL LINK

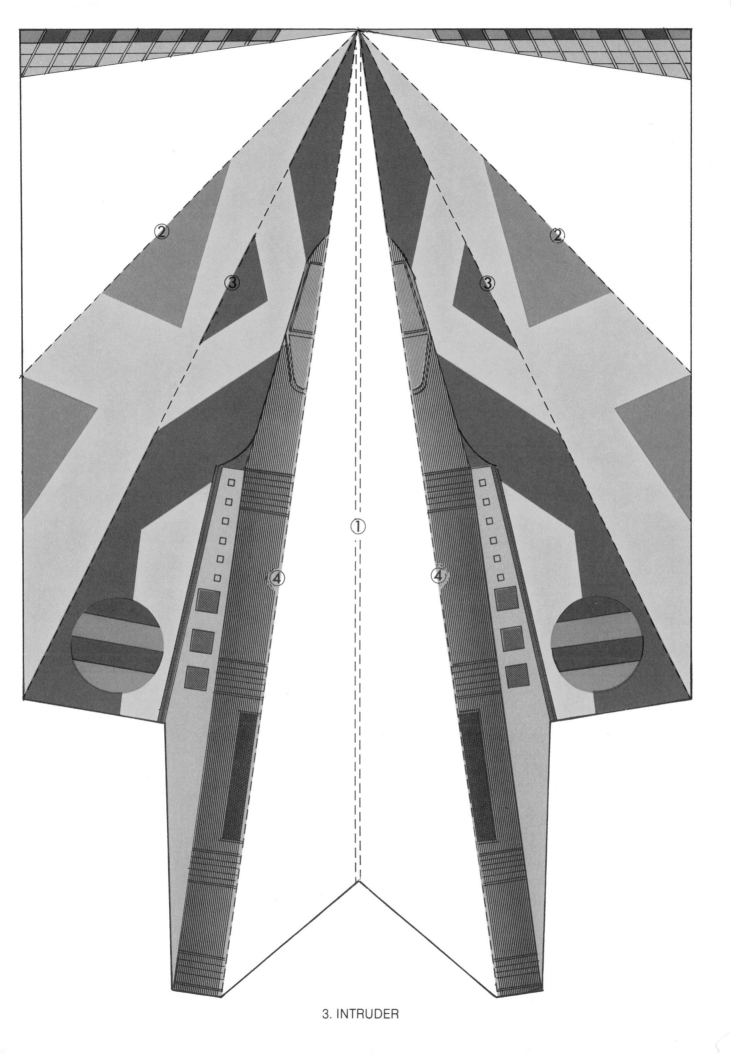

3. INTRUDER

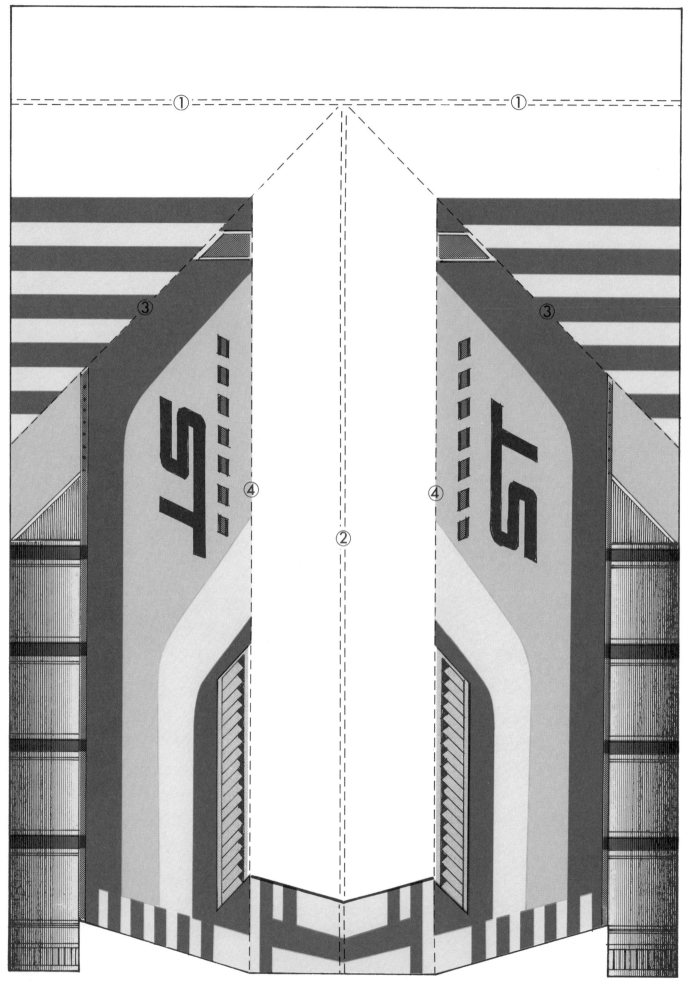

4. STAR TRANSPORTER

5. ROUTEFINDER

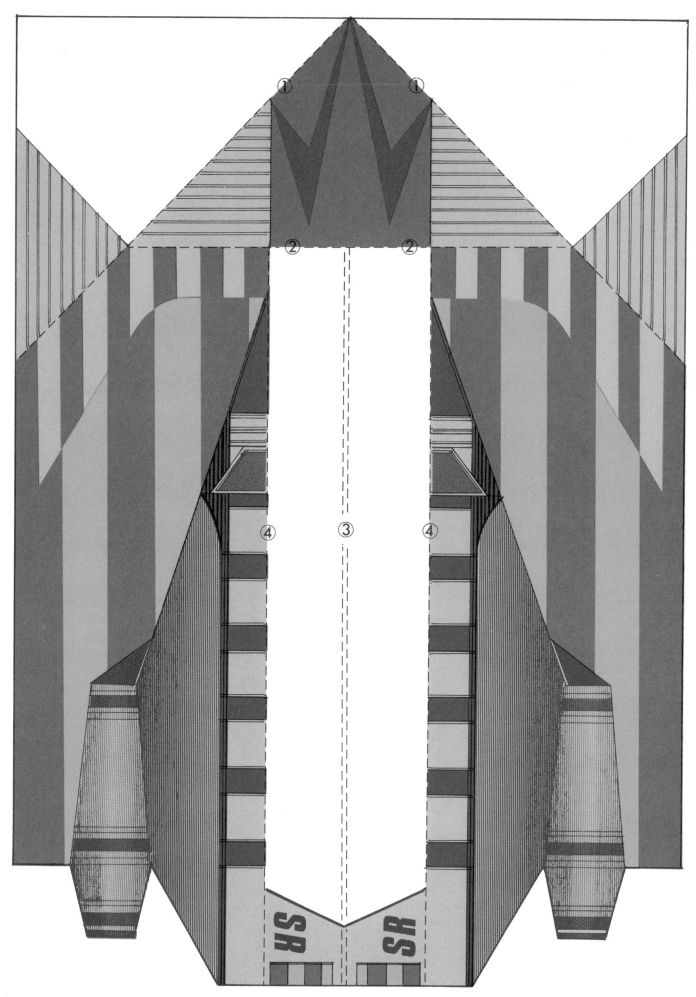

6. SPACE RAM

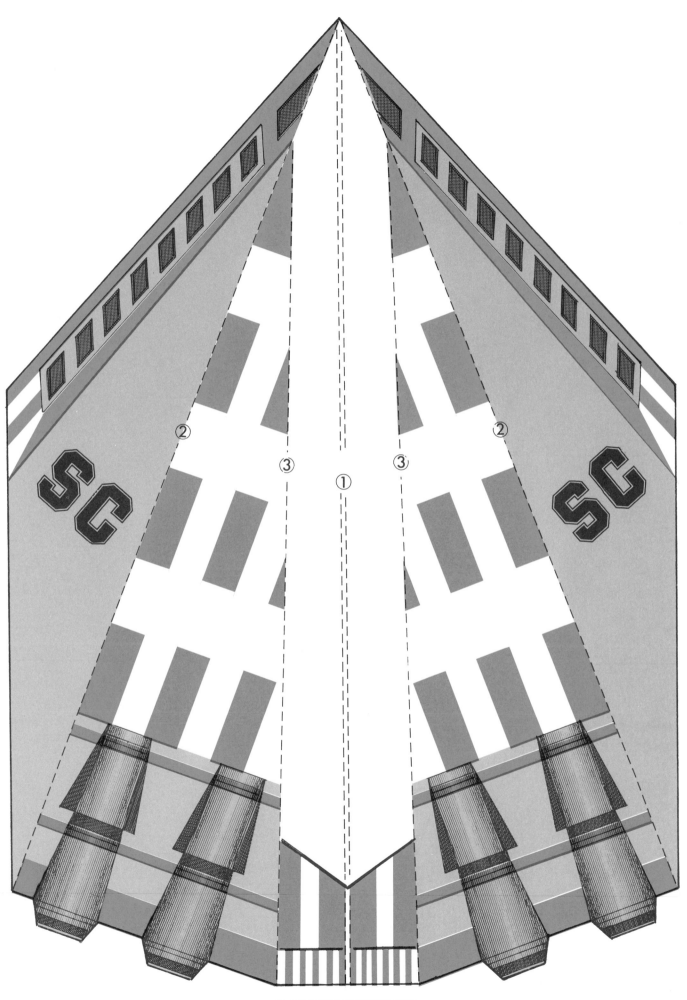

7. SUPERCONTINENTAL

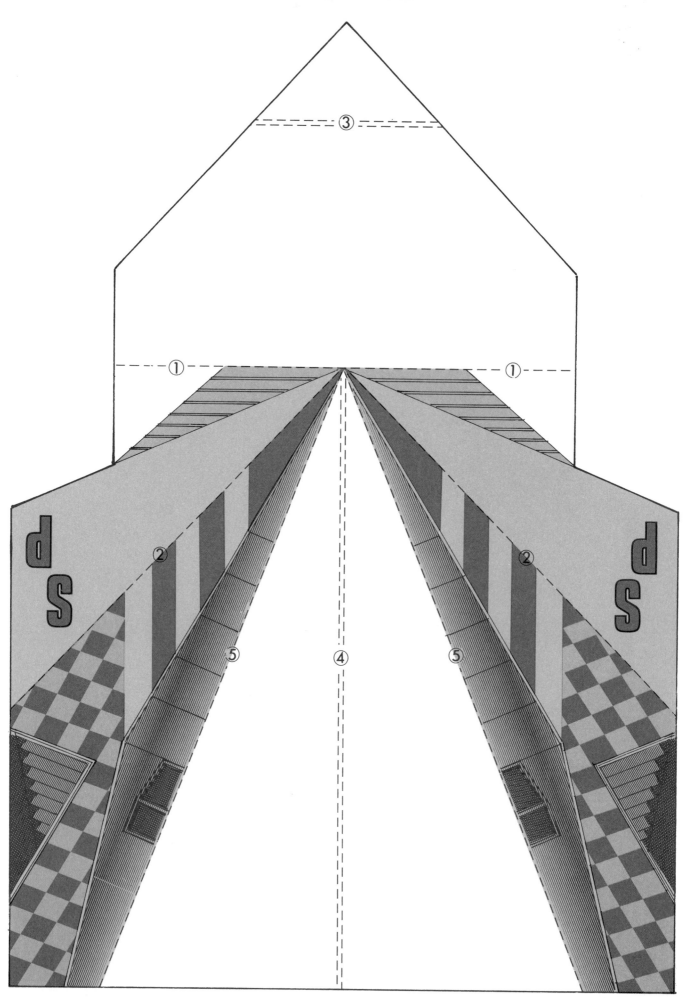

8. STAR PROBE

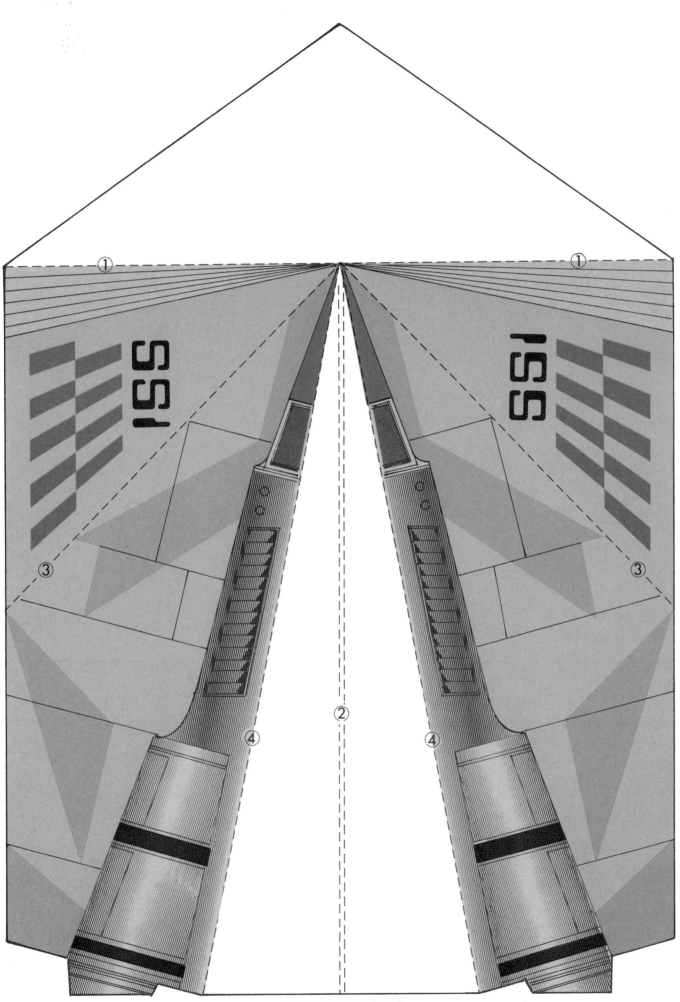

9. SPACE SEARCHER

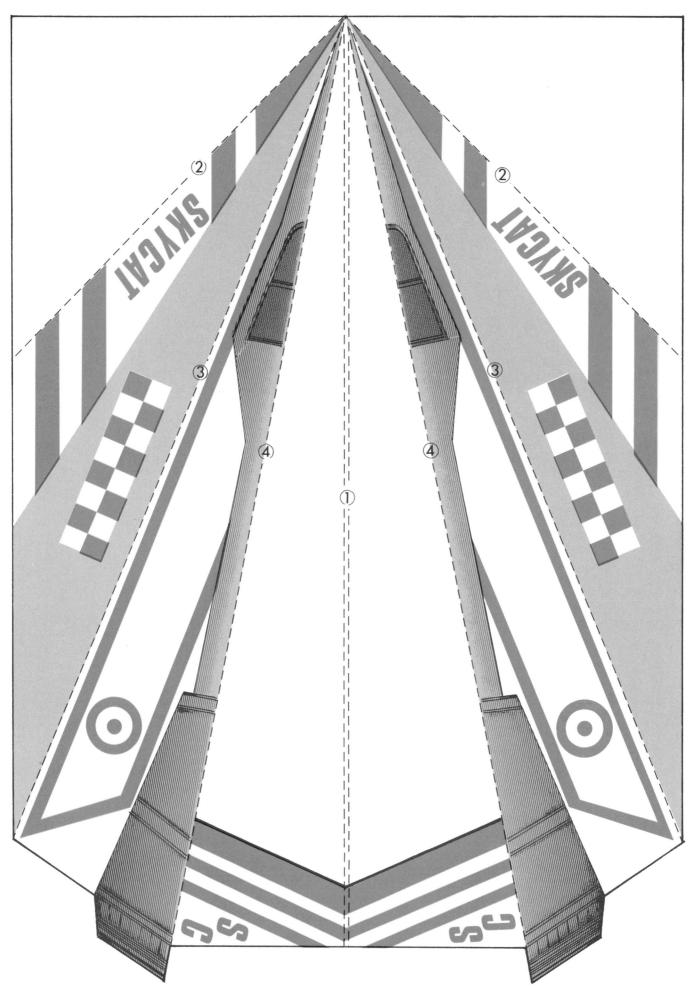

10. SKYCAT

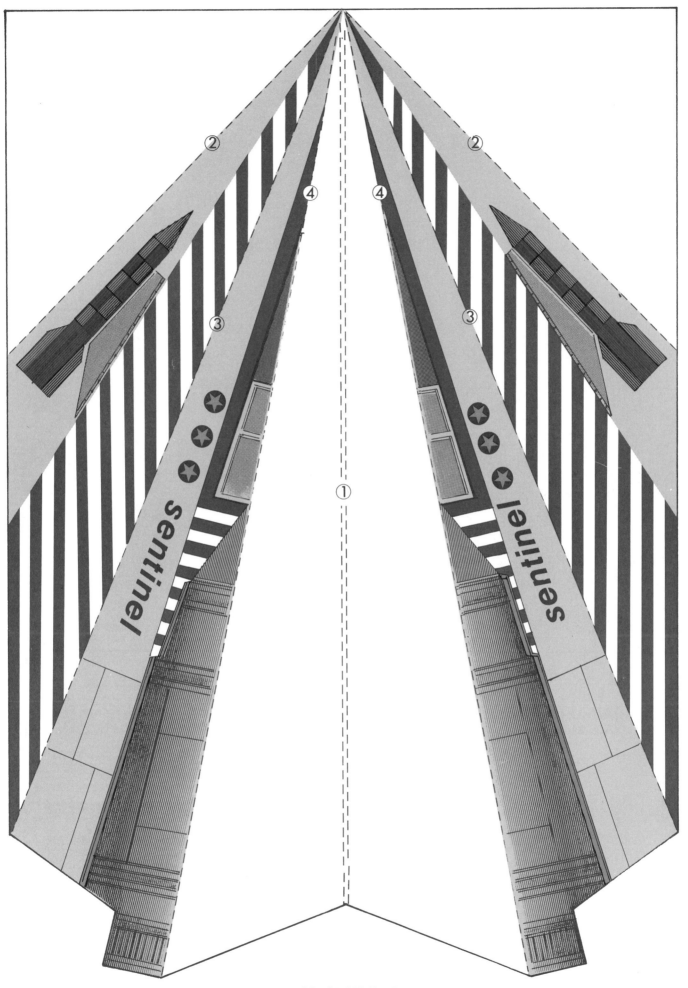

11. SPACE SENTINEL

12. STAR CRUISER

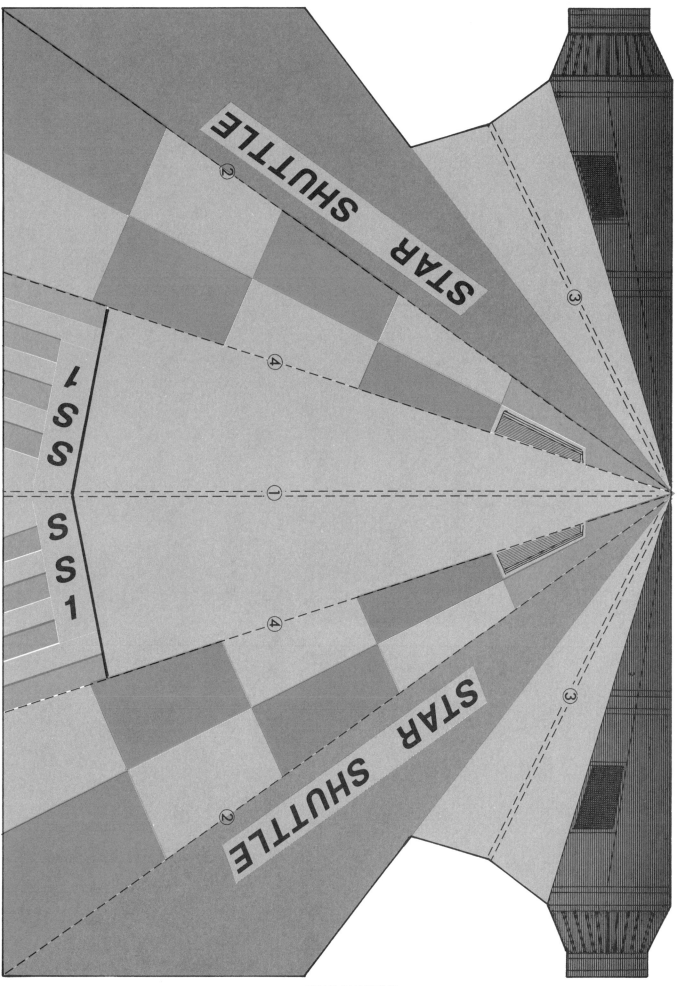

13. STAR SHUTTLE

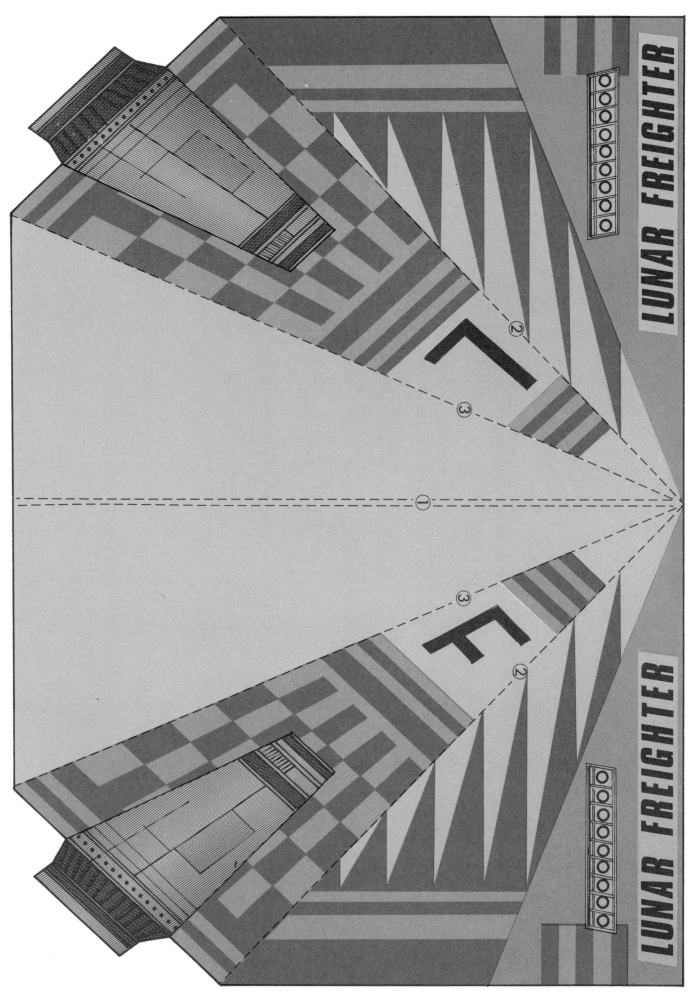

14. LUNAR FREIGHTER

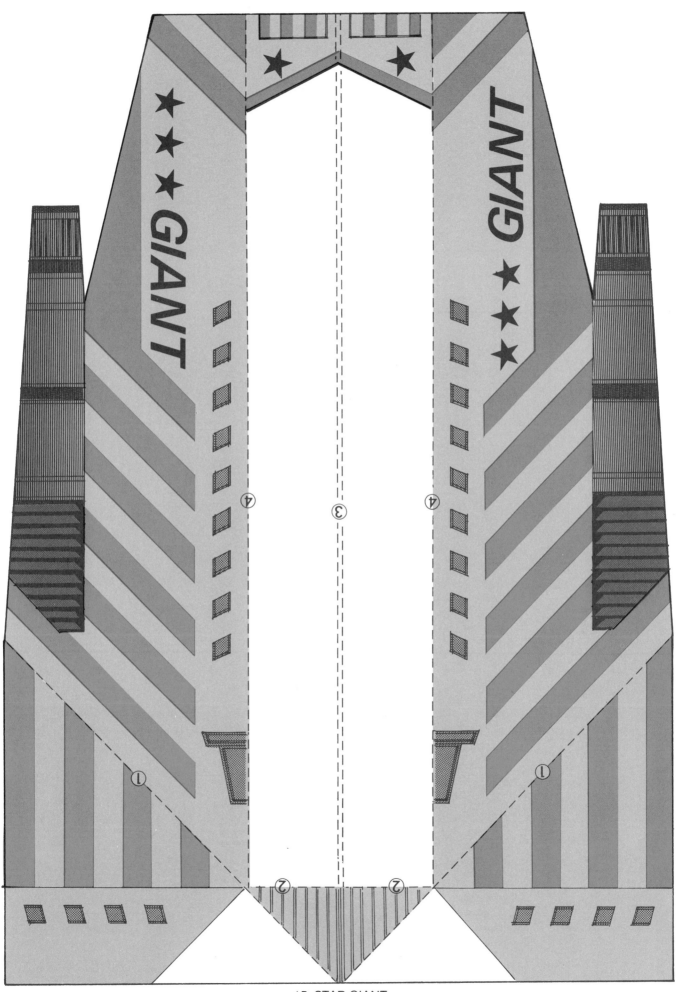

15. STAR GIANT

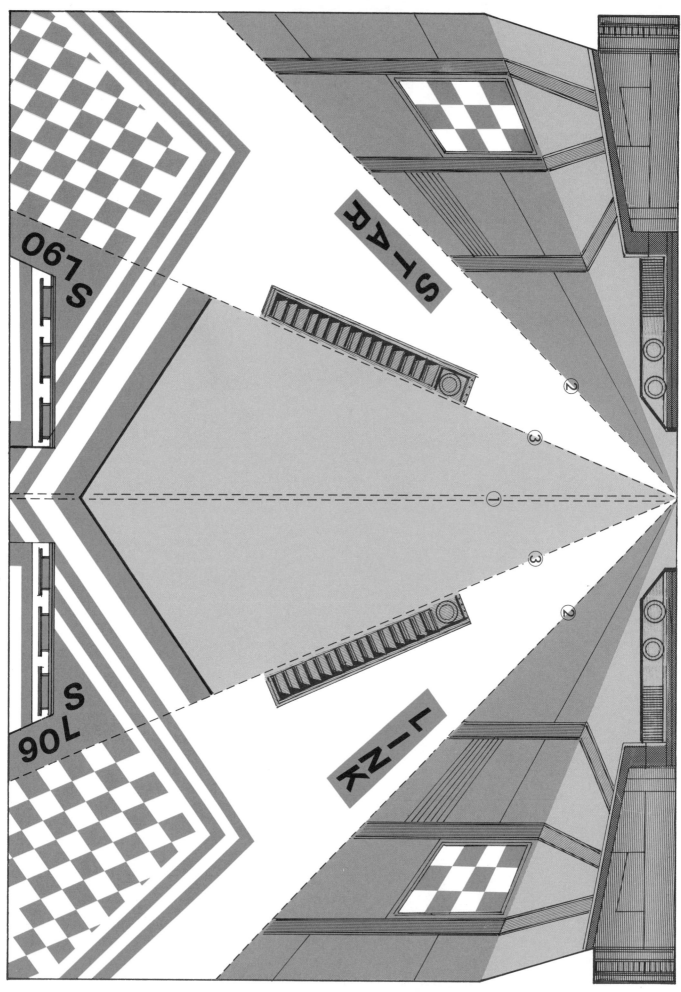

16. STAR LINK

EXPLANATORY DIAGRAMS

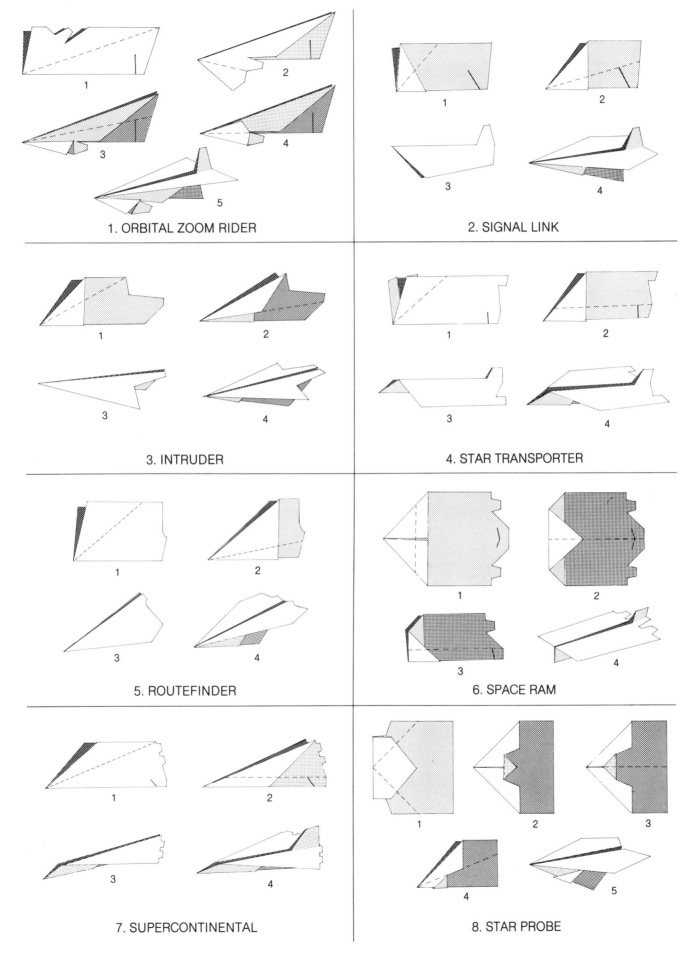

1. ORBITAL ZOOM RIDER

2. SIGNAL LINK

3. INTRUDER

4. STAR TRANSPORTER

5. ROUTEFINDER

6. SPACE RAM

7. SUPERCONTINENTAL

8. STAR PROBE

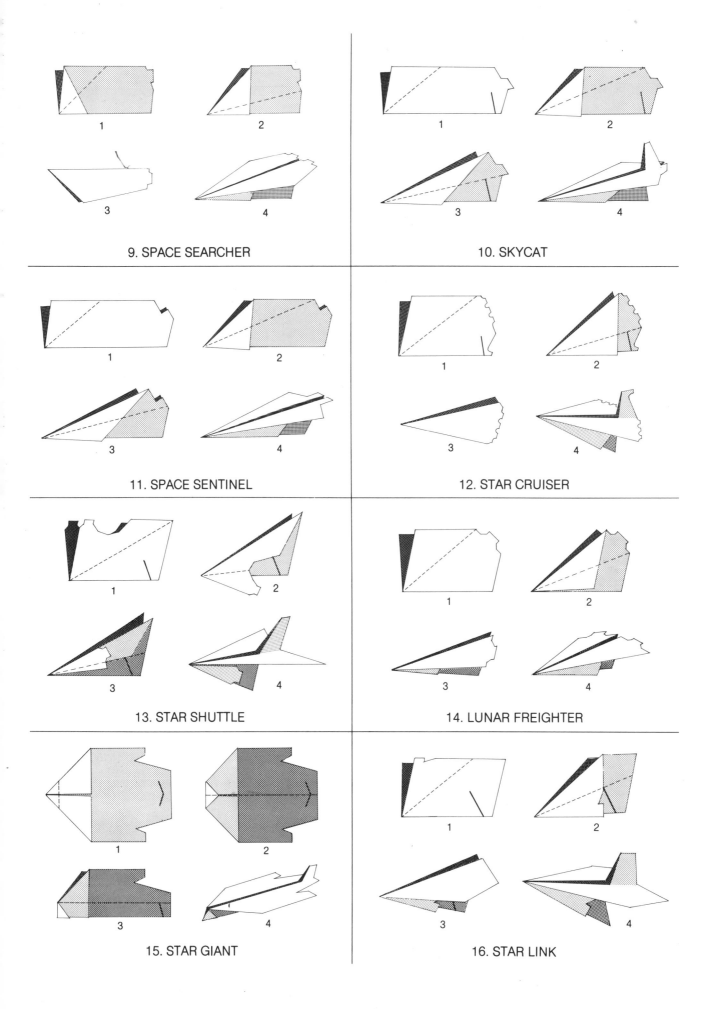

9. SPACE SEARCHER

10. SKYCAT

11. SPACE SENTINEL

12. STAR CRUISER

13. STAR SHUTTLE

14. LUNAR FREIGHTER

15. STAR GIANT

16. STAR LINK